About

St Michael's Mount

Michael Sagar-Fenton

Bossiney Books · Launceston

Contents

This reprint 2008
First published 1999 by Bossiney Books
Langore, Launceston, Cornwall PL15 8LD
© 1999 Michael Sagar-Fenton

ISBN 978-1-899383-19-1

Acknowledgements
The publishers are grateful to the following for permission to reproduce
photographs: Andrew Besley, front cover and pages 4, 24/5 and 41; Lord St
Levan/John Miller/The National Trust, page 17; The National Trust, pages
23, 29, 35 and 40; The National Trust/Andrew Besley, pages 32, 33 and 36;
The National Trust/K Paver, page 11; Penlee House, Gallery and Museum,
Penzance, page 6; Royal Institution of Cornwall, page 18; Paul Watts, pages
8, 20, 21, 28, 39 and 48; West Country Publications Ltd, pages 12/13; Roy
Westlake, pages 42 and 45. The photograph on page 3 is from the author;
all other photographs are from the publishers' own collection.

Printed in Great Britain by R Booth Ltd, Mabe, Cornwall

Lightly clad author on Marazion beach, 1955, with sister Penny on the right. In the background the wreck of HMS Warspite *can be seen between the Hogus and the Mount on a low spring tide*

Introduction – Growing up

To a child even ordinary things are wonderful, and in the same way wonderful things can be quite ordinary. The Cornish world I first became aware of was the huge semi-circle of sea between the arms of Cudden Point to the east and Penzer Point to the west. In the middle of this stood the shallow triangle of St Michael's Mount, crowned by an impeccably logical castle. It never looked extraordinary, but simply just right. It still does, and I know I share this impression with those seeing it for the first time in their lives – there is a fine balance and harmony between the building and its plinth, between Nature and Man.

Other aspects of the beach at the time were perhaps even more remarkable than an island with a castle on top. Between the Mount and the outcrop of rocks to the west called the Hogus stretched the remains of a battleship, a feature which seemed to me as permanent as either.

Not many visitors see the Mount like this, in a blizzard

I was taken from my bed as an infant and held aloft to see the crippled ship driven, like many before her, ashore onto the sands of Marazion. *HMS Warspite* was never to move again. Instead of continuing her final tow to the shipyards of Barry, she became a small industry in our midst. She shrank as I grew, going from a grey mass to a series of rusty lumps, assisted by occasional exciting bouts of dynamiting. A barge made a stately voyage from Penzance at the start of each day and returned with its spoils in the evening. At very low tides you could walk down the wet sands to the wreck itself which even in its last days towered above humans.

The breaking crew visited it at all states of the tide by duck – or rather by DUKW, American open trucks with a wheel at each corner and a propeller at the back which delighted me and everyone else by going straight into the sea and becoming boats

The Mount seen from Chapel Rock where as children we would devise stratagems for capturing the castle

(one remains, serving the Mount as an all-tide transporter). They drove down a beach which still sported rusty grids of scaffolding pipes set at acute angles to the sand, pipes that once covered all the open stretches of seashore to deter potential wartime attempts to land by sea or by glider. They were supposedly cleared away, but the sands of Marazion beach are like the tide itself, capable of rising and falling several metres. In particular they were revealed by the perambulations of the Red River which runs out of the Marsh. As it roamed, it often turned up complexes of decaying poles which served as ideal climbing frames, with the added spice of jagged edges to cut yourself on and a wetting if you fell.

Every midday in the week the air would be filled with a sudden thunder, a physical blow which rattled the windows of our porch. Directly opposite us the quarry of Penlee set off its explosives, and the resonance of its mighty hemisphere projected the sound over three miles of sea to resound more loudly in Marazion than in its neighbouring village of Newlyn. It too was ordinary and so punctual that it formed part of the town's lunchtime rituals.

The river was our playground, and the Folly Fields (which now serve as a car park), and the tennis court (where the children's playground now is) and the Marsh. The variety of birds that visited the Marsh also seemed quite normal, as normal as the numerous solitary men with binoculars who were always peering over the hedges to see them. Only the pelican which escaped from a travelling zoo and lived for several happy years nearby (to the bewilderment of bird watchers) called for comment.

Trains ran through the Marsh on a hidden causeway, shooting under the road bridge to the little station where we loaded boxes of flowers in the summer. After dark their steam was lit

The railway from Penzance opened as far as Redruth in 1852. By 1859 it was possible to reach London, changing gauge at Truro

with red sparks, and the sound of their musical wheels echoed onto the surrounding hills and sang me to sleep at nights.

Despite all these distractions, the main fascination was the Mount itself, and its little cousin Chapel Rock. Chapel Rock was every child's primer in rock climbing and rock pools, with graded exploits suitable for every age. From it you could take cover and examine the Mount at your leisure, reconnoitring and devising stratagems for capturing the castle, as many had before you in earnest. You could watch the changeless sequence of tidal access to the Mount: first the open causeway, second by boat to the causeway landing stage, then to Chapel Rock, then to the landing stage at The Gwelva close to the town square, and finally in deep water to the plain concrete harbour of Top Tieb at the eastern end of the beach. We knew the best and deepest pools, and made boats to sail across them of dry cow parsley with litter sails and scraps of slate stuck in below as a keel.

We also knew all the Mount guides and boatmen, and scrounged shamelessly for a berth in the point of the bow for a free trip to the Mount and back, or on red letter days a trip right round it. We knew the causeway and the best rocks to tip suddenly over to catch unwary crabs. We knew the harbour and village at the Mount's foot. The only place we hardly knew at all was the castle itself and its grounds. They were open infrequently and then, as now, you had to pay. One or two visits, tagged on to strange school parties, were oddly unimpressive. After all, to a child it was only a house, if a big one. The views were wonderful, particularly of the bay, but something was wrong – and it took a while to realise what it was. You couldn't see the Mount.

It seemed better to gaze at it from a distance, lit by the sun or drowned by a storm, or on unforgettable days when blocked out by a low morning mist with only the castle visible, floating on feathers of vapour. Even then it still looked just right.

'It still looked just right...' Many visitors will share this feeling: amazing as the Mount appears at first sight, it seems perfectly at ease in its surroundings

Monastery

As F E Halliday points out in his *History of Cornwall* (Duckworth, 1959), a journey from London to Land's End is a trip back in geological time, at a rate of about a million years per mile. The oldest parts of Britain lie to the extreme west, massive extrusions of granite which pushed up under the buckling surface strata some three hundred million years ago. Some of the durable granite bosses emerged and formed the western boundaries as the softer materials were worn away. One of these was the plateau of West Penwith, and a tiny thumb of this mighty fist poked out through the sheets of slate to form St Michael's Mount.

Perhaps the Mount was once simply a promontory, a cliff, like the carn of about the same height in Marazion known as the Beacon. Either the sea rose or, more likely, the land subsided and the sea washed its sides. Over aeons the neck of land disappeared until the Mount parted company with the mainland altogether and its true shape was slowly sculpted away.

The Mount we are used to is neither island nor mainland, but a tidal island rising two metres (seven feet) from mean low water. The combination of separation and accessibility has made it an irresistible attraction. It gave it unmatched potential as both a defensive retreat and a trading station, a half-way house between land and sea.

There has been a long and learned argument over the reputed Cornish name of the Mount: 'Carrek Los Yn Cos', The Grey Rock in the Wood. The phrase leads to the idea that the Mount deserved this romantic description at some time in recent human history, and the bay was then suddenly inundated. However, the weight of evidence is against this, and it is far more probable that the name originally applied to Mont St Michel in Normandy whose history the Mount shares in so many other ways. The 'wood' certainly still exists in Marazion, although now only in the dark carboniferous sand and the occasional petrified log revealed by a once-in-a-lifetime storm.

History relies on written records, and there are none relating to the early days of the Mount. It must have existed for millennia as a stubby rock covered in gorse and heather, but from their first awareness men and women cannot have failed to appreciate its advantages as a stronghold, a quiet courting place, a look-out to spot enemies, or for peering through the squalls for the sudden bounty of a shipwreck. In an exposed bay its sheltered side must also have provided a safe sandy place to land a boat and so must have been the focus of its local community from the beginning.

When history finally does take note of the Mount for the first time, it is not as a strange primitive backwater but as a full-blown trading post, the centre of a community which the writer Diodorus Siculus asserts approvingly was 'fond of strangers, civilised in their manners through intercourse with foreign merchants'. Diodorus's account is of the voyage of Pytheas in the 4th century BC in which the Mount is described as 'Ictis'. The method of streaming for tin and the details of its transport over to the Mount at low water are all faithfully recorded. It is likely the Mount was the first and most important port in Cornwall, and so it must have remained for several hundred years. The Roman invasion came and went, and touched little of West Cornwall, though the trade in tin probably continued via the Mount.

The next glimpse we have of the Mount's strategic importance is not until the era of the Celtic saints. The Saxons had taken over most of Britain, driving the Christian Celtic communities to the fringes as well as to Brittany and Ireland. Their route to each other's territory was a fraught sea journey, of which the passage to Land's End was by far the most dangerous. They therefore chose West Penwith as a necessary stopover,

'A lookout to spot enemies or to peer through the squalls for the sudden bounty of a shipwreck'

using Hayle on the north coast and the Mount on the south, with a short and easy land crossing from one side to the other. The Saints – a legendary group of eccentric and sometimes quarrelsome Celtic missionaries – made their mark on Cornwall, especially on its place names. It is said there are more saints in the county than there are in heaven. No doubt during this period the first of many places of worship was erected on the top of the granite outcrop on the peak of the island.

Following the saints came the pilgrims, and with them the foundation for the Mount's role for many years. Penance and absolution, which were necessary in order to enter heaven, required those who could afford it to make extravagant journeys of pilgrimage. St Michael's Mount was a natural disembarking place for such expeditions, and gradually itself became a place of pilgrimage. The economic advantages of a steady stream of self-selectingly wealthy visitors needing food, shelter and the other essentials and comforts of life were not lost on the locals.

All that was lacking was a miraculous apparition, and it is hardly surprising that in 495 a group of fishermen reported a vision of St Michael standing on one of the rocky outcrops on the western side of the island. Sanctified by this, the Mount's main purpose changed from a trading port (although it stayed as such) to one of the more important locations in Christendom.

For several centuries little changed. Through the offices of St Augustine the Saxons were converted to Christianity and reunited with Rome, and by gradual degrees the warring tribes of England were welded into a single nation. Cornwall was marginalised, since it was not considered worth the trouble of marching a large army so far just to capture it. It was Egbert who finally came west and brought Cornwall into the English nation in 838. By then the chief danger was not from land, but from sea – the coastal skirmishes with the Danes were a feature of the next two hundred years. Few major intrusions are recorded, but Mount's Bay must have been too great a temptation – not to mention a safe anchorage – to have been ignored by the Danes, and the inhabitants must have lived in constant fear of the sea.

During this time the little religious community maintained its hold, aided by gifts from pilgrims, by small endowments of land and by tithes, particularly fish. This thin stream of income kept the Mount through many a bad time. Not usually enough to be worth fighting over, but enough to be significant and desirable, it made the Mount self-sufficient in a way that its twenty-four acres of bony granite would never have allowed.

The dark ages of St Michael's Mount ended with the Norman invasion. The Normans lost little time in making an inventory of their new conquest, and Cornwall did not escape their thorough examination. Eventually William the Conqueror bestowed most of the county upon his half-brother Robert, Count of Mortain. In his turn, and conscious of his immortal soul, Robert gave St Michael's Mount along with half a hide of land (384 acres) and the right to hold a market on Thursdays to the great Benedictine abbey of Mont St Michel in Normandy.

A tiny village which existed simply to serve the Mount established itself opposite, and became known as 'Marghas Yow' – 'Thursday market'. Another settlement close by earned the name of 'Little Market' or 'Marghas Byghan', and from these come 'Market Jew' (which still exists in 'Market Jew Street' in Penzance) and 'Marazion'. Despite the obvious connotations in these names, they are both corruptions of the Cornish and have no known Jewish connection.

Mont St Michel is on a far more magnificent scale than St Michael's Mount, although it occupies a remarkably similar offshore tidal site. Since France and England were now combined, other grants of land were given by the conquerors to both institutions, and in 1135 the Abbot of the French Mount established a Benedictine priory on St Michael's Mount as a subsidiary of his own. The two were administered as one body. The Cornish Mount was considered sufficiently important to have gained from Pope Gregory VII the privilege of conferring on all pilgrims who visited it with alms and oblations the remission of one third of their penance – no small amount, and a favour which has never been withdrawn to this day.

The religious life was the main business of the Mount, but this often went hand in hand with military business, and the Mount's advantages as a military stronghold were not ignored. These were put to the test in 1193 by a supporter of John, Earl of Cornwall (later King John), called Henry de la Pomeroy. With Richard the Lionheart secure in an Austrian prison, John attempted to take the crown of England, and de la Pomeroy played his part by seizing the Mount. He disguised his men as pilgrims who, on a prearranged signal, threw back their cloaks and showed their weapons and chain mail beneath. The abbey surrendered without a fight and the Mount was held by the invaders for over a year. However, the unexpected ransom and return of the King upset all their plans and de la Pomeroy yielded without resistance to an army led by the Archbishop of Canterbury, Hubert Walter. De la Pomeroy died shortly afterwards, and the Mount resumed its religious role.

From the days of King John onwards there was seldom peace between England and France for long. The unity between the two Mounts of St Michael continued, but in time of war the payments made by the Cornish Mount to the French were suspended, and restored again whenever hostilities ceased. The contemplative life of the little island continued for the next two hundred years while war, plague and history swirled around it. It was broken only by one event of real significance:

Inter horam diei primam et tertiam, factus est . . . terraemotus, Ecclesia . . . sancti Michaelis de Monte . . . cecedit complanata.

Reading like a modern news broadcast, the report of total destruction of the church by an earthquake in 1275 stands alone, a shocking event that still gives cause for reflection. The church which had been consecrated in 1144 was no more. No record of another exists before the 14th century when the main parts of the present church were built, but the business of the priory certainly went on as before.

Marazion gradually established itself as a village in its own

'The Vision of St Michael to the Fishermen', as painted in 1979 by John Miller, hangs in the picture gallery

right, although it was still under the parochial government of St Hilary. A chapel was built on the small granite island (perhaps still attached to the mainland) on which pilgrims to the Mount waited for the tide or the ferry and it became known as Chapel Rock.

The Mount also had a village that waxed and waned, a world away from the priory above, concerned only with fishing and trade. The first actual harbour is recorded in 1320, but the haven and port had been established since before the days of

The village on St Michael's Mount, as it was in 1900. Its origins lie in pre-history, and its population has varied greatly over the years. Some trading vessels probably beached on the Marazion sands, but the Mount offered shelter in a south-west gale, when Marazion is a dangerous lee shore

Ictis, probably equipped with just a wooden jetty. The harbours of Newlyn and Penzance were still unknown, and only Mousehole offered similar shelter and facilities. So the Mount was the centre of maritime activity in the whole of the bay.

The bond between the two priories of Mont St Michel and St Michael's Mount was continually weakened by suspensions of payments during wartime. When in 1408 Henry IV decided it would be better for the revenues to be put towards his own private household expenses, rather than wasted overseas, there was not much opposition. All links were finally severed during the reign of Henry V: St Michael's Mount became an independent institution for the first time. The long peaceable religious association was over, and the Mount, a piece of property with an income attached, became a transferable asset at the whim of its new masters.

Henry V gifted the Mount to his recently established Syon Abbey at Twickenham, but Henry VI snatched it back again and for some time it was part of the foundation of his new College of St Nicholas (later King's College), Cambridge. Syon Abbey did not take this lying down, but it was twenty years before the Mount was restored to them. It was worth fighting for, since besides the income of £33 6s 8d (in 1437) the church had a quantity of treasure and plate, and a collection of holy relics – 'Milk of St Marie the Virgin; jawbone of St Mansuetus; arm bone of St Felix; jawbone of St Appolonia; stones from the holy sepulchre; portion of girdle of the Blessed Virgin Mary; fragment of finger-bone of St Agapitt', etc.

The strategic advantages of the Mount caused another intrusion into its privacy at the end of the Wars of the Roses. With a force of some eighty men the Lancastrian Earl of Oxford took the Mount, once again under the pretence of being pilgrims. This time the resulting siege was well defended, aided by the co-operative nature of the Sheriff of Cornwall, Sir Henry Bodrugan, who insisted in a gentlemanly manner on keeping the rebels victualled. Sir John Arundell of Trerice had led the besieging army, but was cut down in a fierce skirmish on the sands beside the causeway. After a certain amount of attrition – mainly between the besieging forces – the Earl's men were tempted into a number of truces and negotiations, and one by one most were lured away by bribes. As the scholar John Warkworth said, 'there is a proverb that a castle which speaketh and a woman that will hear, they will be gotten both', and so the Earl was eventually left with less than a dozen followers. After a long winter's resistance, he surrendered to Richard Fortescue who had replaced Bodrugan as Sheriff.

In such times of tension at home and abroad, the Mount's function was changing from spiritual house of worship and learning to fortified stronghold. This was tested again when a party of marauding French soldiers landed in Marazion with the intention of taking the Mount – perhaps, as they saw it, taking it back. It had never yet been captured by storm, and once more its natural advantages came to its rescue. The skirmishing party was beaten off, but retaliated by burning Marazion to the ground before escaping.

The Mount's access to the high seas gave it a value far in excess of a landlocked castle. No longer could it exist as a sparsely defended priory. Soldiers and clergy could probably have continued side by side for many years to come, but Henry VIII was now on the throne and his personal needs as well as his mistrust of Rome led him to radical solutions. Unable to bring the monasteries under his control, he simply did the unthinkable and made away with them, distributing their lands amongst his friends. Among them was Syon Abbey, dissolved in 1539, and with it St Michael's Mount.

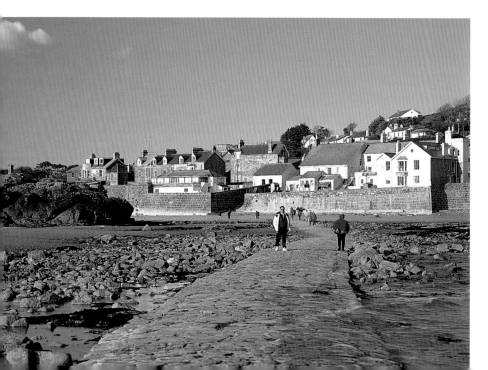

Above: The Mount harbour

Opposite: Marazion from the Causeway

Fortress

For strategic reasons the Mount was considered too important to meet the same fate as that of so many of its fellow priories. The buildings were not pulled down, and to our great gain the 14th-century church (whose foundations may have survived the 1275 earthquake and dated from the time of the Conquest) still stands as the centrepiece of the castle. But the faithful line of clergy whose attendance had lasted unbroken for a thousand years were sent away.

The property was leased to the Milliton family of Pengersick, so long as they repaired the buildings and the pier, and supported a garrison of five soldiers. The great banqueting hall on the north-eastern meadows, which appears as a feature in all contemporary pictures, fell into disrepair and was eventually pulled down – its foundations were rediscovered during drainage work in 1994.

The new defences were soon to see action. The Cornish had little sentimental affection for the monks and their doings, but they were utterly incensed by the changes forced upon them in their parish churches. In particular the abandonment of the Latin mass and its replacement by an English prayer book led to violent dissent.

Their reasonable argument was that English was equally as foreign to them as Latin, and that if they could not have a Cornish prayer book they would stay with the words made familiar to generations of their forebears. The rebellions of An Gof and Perkin Warbeck were still within living memory, and revolution still smouldered in the air. The appointed governor of the Mount was another Arundell – Humphrey – and he joined the rebel cause.

Across the West Country there was a general rising, and the alarmed gentry with their wives and children sought sanctuary

The old and the very old – the Victorian extension on the left blends seemlessly into the original fortress on the right

Overleaf: The sight of the castle by moonlight can be breathtakingly romantic

in any defended place, the Mount amongst them. They were immediately surrounded – Arundell came down in person to lead the seige on the Mount.

Again it resisted direct assault, but the lower slopes were soon taken.

By the ingenious strategy of carrying large bales of hay as a defensive shield, which were later set alight and used as smoke screens, the attackers tightened their grip. The ill-prepared and frightened occupants were quickly brought to terms. Happily no massacre took place, and the terrified families were despatched to the rebel headquarters at Bodmin. Like the other rebellions, this too was crushed, and Arundell was eventually hanged at Tyburn.

During the later 16th century the shifts of power and fortune between the three principal nations of England, France and Spain dominated all else. Queen Elizabeth played a diplomatic hand with the Spanish catholics, while her navy were given licence as legalised pirates to harass and rob them at every opportunity. They retaliated in kind. Cornwall was in the front line, and all its fortifications were strengthened and extended. The tin trade had also revived, and the increasing population led to considerable growth of the communities at Mousehole, Newlyn, Penzance and Marazion, as well as the village on the Mount. No longer did the Mount have claim to be the only port of significance in the bay, although its fortifications ensured it was still the most vital.

At last the patience of the Spanish was exhausted and invasion forces were made ready. In July 1588 the beacon on the Mount flared in warning as the vast Spanish fleet drifted up the English Channel to its ill-fated encounter with Howard, Drake and the English weather.

Cheated of England, the Spanish invaded Brittany, an ideal base from which to sally forth in raids on channel shipping. In 1595 a raiding party went further and landed in Mount's Bay, burning Paul, Mousehole, Newlyn and Penzance, and staying ashore for a couple of nights. They sensibly decided that the Mount would be too big a bone to chew, and they escaped on a fair wind before Drake could make the passage of the Lizard to catch them. Marazion was the largest community left standing,

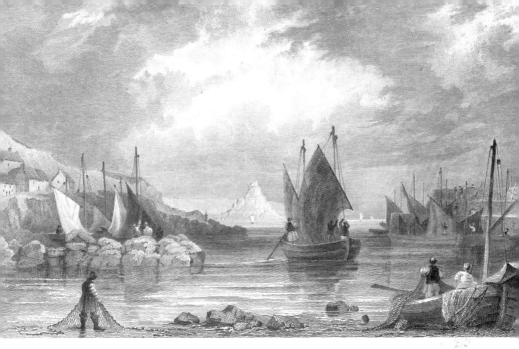

At Mousehole, a medieval fishing port, a quay was under construction as early as 1393, but its trading activities were limited almost entirely to importing salt and exporting fish. Its population grew during the Tudor period

just five weeks after its Royal Charter had been granted by the Queen.

Warfare and siege are expensive pursuits, and Elizabeth was forced to review all her assets. In 1599 many church lands were sold by the crown into private hands, and amongst them was the Mount which became a piece of transferable property open to the highest bidder.

It was bought by Robert Cecil, later Earl of Salisbury, but it is doubtful if he even set foot there, and the Mount continued to be leased to Sir Arthur Harris, an indefatigable man under whose command the garrison and defences were kept in excellent order. In a contemporary view it appears an impregnable place indeed – a walled castle surrounds the church at the top, a single track leads down to a few poor fishermen's huts and

For those who live or work on the Mount, the ferry to Marazion can be a wet and windy business

Opposite: Looking up from the seaward side – 'an unassailable bastion'

then the enclosed harbour. On the sea side of the Mount (which is rarely illustrated), the rock face rises almost sheer from the apron of land around shore – an unassailable bastion.

It needed to be, for as the threat from Spain reduced so the influence of the Dutch increased and, even more dangerous for the Cornish coasts, the north African pirates from Salee and Algiers began to use the Western Approaches as their hunting grounds. They were formidable opponents offshore, but also became feared as raiders, taking hostages to sell into slavery – they were reputed to have abducted a whole churchful of sixty souls, women and children amongst them.

The Earl of Salisbury sold the Mount in 1640 to Sir Francis Bassett who later became Sheriff of Cornwall. This was the year in which Charles I recalled Parliament from its long absence to pay for his wars with the Scots, a parliament which was shortly to carry the Grand Remonstrance declaring no confidence in the king. Two years after acquiring the Mount, Bassett found himself embroiled in the civil war as one of the king's most faithful soldiers.

Cornwall was instinctively royalist, and during the early heady days of the civil war Bassett was at the fore of the successful battles fought all over the West Country as far as Bristol. Eventually, however, Fairfax's army beat remorselessly westwards. The Prince of Wales, later Charles II, spent a few days at the Mount before setting sail for Scilly. The Mount was a prize the royalists were reluctant to surrender, as it had been crucial in importing arms and ammunition from France (Bassett himself had spent over £1500 of his own money on its garrison).

In March 1646 Lord Hopton surrendered to the parliamentary forces in Truro, but refused to include Pendennis Castle or the Mount, instead sending two hundred men under Sir Arthur Bassett (who had succeeded his brother, Francis) to the Mount to defend it. However, the cause was already lost and Sir Arthur had little heart for resistance. Despite being well armed and having ample provisions, Bassett negotiated a surrender of the Mount on 16 April.

The Bassetts were not deprived of the Mount after Cromwell's victory, but they were made to pay swingeing fines and, despite their tin revenues, were forced to part with it in 1659. To make it harder to swallow, the purchaser was a prominent parliamentarian, a certain John St Aubyn of Clowance who had been appointed Captain of the Mount by parliament after the war. St Aubyn had taken on the duties of the Mount with relish. Despite their previous loyalties, the St Aubyns' tenure survived the restoration of the monarchy. The family

The inhabitants of Mount's Bay acquired a sinister reputation as 'wreckers'. Certainly any ship which came ashore was likely to be broken up by the people before it was broken up by the sea, but there is no evidence of deliberate luring of sailors to their deaths

came through many other vicissitudes during the next three hundred years, but remained custodians of the Mount – as they are today.

Country House

After the departure of its last garrison of soldiers in 1660, the Mount was in a poor state. The church had been used as a magazine, and had narrowly escaped being pulled down altogether – its demolition had been ordered by Hopton in 1645 but never executed, although the ruined remains of St Catherine's Chapel on Chapel Rock were destroyed. The St Aubyns did not yet choose to exchange the sheltered meadows of Clowance for the exposed and half-ruined Mount as their residence, but they did set willingly about its restoration.

With the end of the international and civil hostilities and the beginning of the golden age of tin and copper exploration, there was time and money available. Amongst their early improvements was the famous frieze in the 'Chevy Chase' room, the monks' old refectory.

Left: The blue drawing room. Its many attractive features include 'Gothick' rococo plaster-work, portraits by Cornish painter John Opie, and Chippendale chairs

Opposite: The beautiful Chevy Chase room. The name comes from a plaster frieze of hunting scenes running around the room

Mount's Bay was prospering and the harbour on the Mount was no longer the only or prime port. The delicate manoeuvring required to make the harbour mouth under sail – especially in a stiff sou'wester – must have led to many a grounding on the shores of Marazion, and the quiet corner of the bay occupied by Newlyn and Penzance was a powerful counter-attraction. Under the St Aubyns the Mount harbour was enlarged and then enlarged again.

William Borlase mentions only one resident, a widow by the name of Orchard, living in the Mount village in 1702, but in 1726 a determined attempt was made to re-establish a formal village there. Marazion and the Mount had always had a bad press as places to inhabit. John Leland (c1540) describes Marazion as a 'poore towne', and a certain John Taylor who had travelled all the way from London to see the Mount was sorely disappointed, deeming it 'not worth the taking or keeping, a barren stony little wen or wart'. A prominent Penzance man described Marazion in 1751 as a 'little smuggling town, not worth mentioning', while James Boswell, visiting the Mount in 1792, lamented that it was 'a disgusting shame to have a parcel of low dirty people collected there'. He urged the Baronet to make his surroundings more respectable and to 'remove the town'.

Whatever the state of the village, the castle was going from strength to strength. Borlase was delighted with the improvements to the accommodation, including the restoration of the ruined Lady Chapel as two drawing rooms. Much of the Mount as we know it was shaped in this time as the former barracks and older priory were gradually turned into a country house fit for gentry to settle in.

Opposite: The private entrance to the castle leading to the granite spiral staircase

A restored eighteenth-century barge, rowed by boatmen in their ceremonial livery

The south-eastern terraces were laid out as gardens out of the way of the prevailing winds. The Civil War fortifications were not removed, and many of the defensive works remain today.

The St Aubyns lived the lives of English gentlefolk, mostly following careers in the army and parliament, and many distinguishing themselves in their military exploits. An exception was the fifth baronet, who was better known as a patron of the arts – in particular as a sponsor of the Cornish artist John Opie – and for having fathered fifteen illegitimate children mainly by a local girl whom he eventually married.

The south-western face – the door through which visitors enter the castle

The visit of Queen Victoria in 1846 was a great event for Mount's Bay. The Queen stepped ashore on the Mount from her yacht, and her footprint was preserved in the form of a brass plaque (see the photograph opposite)

The fifth baronet's debts nearly led to the family's ruin, but they weathered the storm without having to part with the Mount. The family's affection for the arts continued down the years, and is expressed not only in an important art collection but also in continuing support and encouragement of living artists.

The Napoleonic wars led to a renewal of tension and a further round of fortification. Twenty years earlier a privateer commanded by a notorious Irish pirate had been fired on from the Mount while chasing a brig into the bay, but sadly the long disuse of the guns caused one of them to explode, killing a young Mount resident, Martin Matthews. The guns spoke again

Victoria's visit to the Mount was commemorated by a brass footprint let in to the granite at the top of the harbour steps

in 1812 when a French frigate was driven ashore, and some of her cannon were retrieved to stand on the upper terraces.

Another sustained effort was made to establish the village around the harbour and for a while it seemed likely to challenge its fellow at the other end of the causeway.

In its heyday it boasted three streets, a school supported by two smaller dames' schools, and no less than three pubs – the Ship Inn, the Shipwrights Arms, and the St Aubyn Arms. This last is supposed to have been closed down when one of its patrons, clearly the worse for wear, failed to give due respect to King Edward VII during a royal visit in 1902.

Most of the business of the village was fishing, especially for pilchards, although many men doubled as boatmen and estate workers, and there was indeed a shipwright on the island for a while. The population peaked at about three hundred souls.

Marazion itself was declining as a fishing port, but benefited from being the mainland base of the St Aubyns' considerable estates, and from the toll from the fine turnpikes at either end of the village. In 1892 it freed itself from nearby St Hilary and became a parish in its own right, although the Mount remained an independent parish, one of the smallest in the country. At length, despite further extension of the harbour, Penzance won the industrial supremacy of Mount's Bay and Newlyn claimed the fishing fleet.

The coming of the railway sealed the process. Marazion became a genteel resort, and the village on the Mount finally succumbed to the continual inconvenience of being marooned for sixteen hours out of every twenty-four. It lost all pretence of any independent existence, and became a model estate whose only purpose was the service of the castle.

Opposite: The view from The Beacon above Marazion

Below: This service tramway was installed during the restoration of the castle by Piers St Aubyn in the 1860s

The causeway was not properly laid until 1898. Until then it was just a natural shingle bank

Towards the end of the Victorian period the castle took another huge step. Sir John St Aubyn, later the first Lord St Levan, commissioned his cousin Piers St Aubyn to design a substantial extension to enlarge and improve the cold and draughty accommodation of the house. His brief was to do so without spoiling or greatly altering the outline of the Mount which had survived for so many centuries.

This was achieved by cunningly 'tucking in' what amounts to a sizable country house on the sheer south-eastern side, a feat best appreciated from the sea. A large wooden staging was erected to bring materials up to the summit, and a second roadway was laid to a new entrance at the bottom of a granite spiral staircase. A tunnel was dug by miners to contain a service tramway at about the same time. It was by general agreement a triumph of restrained craftsmanship which married to the original buildings as happily as those buildings co-existed with the crag itself.

The family abandoned Clowance, and continued to make improvements to their now stately home. The model dairy, a copy of the larger one at Glastonbury Abbey, with its fine granite roof was built in 1870 to serve the island's herd of six Jersey cows. A small wood was planted which gave the Mount a new profile until the blizzard in 1987 and the hurricane of 1990 reduced it so greatly. New planting has since taken place.

The village finally fell to the fate envisaged by Boswell and was mostly removed, to be rebuilt in its current form. The St Aubyn Arms still survives, as well as the fish cellar which is now the restaurant, the laundry which now serves as the cafe, and a number of other individual dwellings. The new terrace – Elizabeth Terrace – was laid out, and the rest of the buildings tidied up to form the compact and formal settlement seen today.

The causeway was also properly laid for the first time in 1898, having consisted previously of a line of shingle laid naturally by the confluence of the tides meeting around the island. A wall was constructed to protect the castle and gardens from the railway-borne tourists who had begun to flock across to the harbour. At length the Jersey herd was sent away and, with the final eradication of the ancient rabbit warren, the Mount abandoned all attempts at self-sufficiency.

The two World Wars brought little change, except an influx

of troops and a group of three concrete pill-boxes, the latest in the Mount's agglomeration of defensive works stretching back to prehistory.

In the 1950s the St Aubyn family decided to take a serious look at the alternative prospects for the Mount's future.

Commercialisation was an obvious possibility, since there was an ever-expanding and largely unexploited tourist market at hand, but the family balked at the change in the character of the place which would have ensued (for comparison, visit the cacophonous tourist shopping street which ascends present-day Mont St Michel).

At the time, Lord St Levan was brother-in-law to the writer Harold Nicolson, then chairman of The National Trust. Nicolson's celebrated wife, Vita Sackville-West, was also involved in The National Trust and had created the famous garden at Sissinghurst in Kent. The family were immensely impressed at the standards being set by The Trust in the field of conservation, and eventually resolved to gift the Mount to the nation by donating it to the organisation, together with a large endowment fund for its upkeep. They retained only the Victorian wing and some of the gardens on a 999-year lease for their own private use.

This historic gift gave The National Trust a picturesque flagship which did much to raise its profile in the following years. It swiftly became one of its most visited locations (it is still currently third).

The castle and older parts of the house were opened to the public, though the 19th-century house, including the kitchens and one of the most romantically-set dining rooms in the world, remains the family's private quarters. About 200,000 people visit the castle every year, and probably three times as many again cross the causeway to walk around the harbour.

Above: The lure of walking to the Mount at low tide is irresistible

Below: Mont St Michel in Normandy

Past and Future

History alone cannot adequately explain the appeal of the Mount.

Artists – from Turner to the cartoonist Giles – have set up their easels on various parts of Marazion beach and even on boats to pay their tribute to its visual perfection. It has been depicted in calm weather and in storms, in sunlight and moonlight, and with a variety of vessels surrounding it, although it is nearly always shown taller and steeper than it truly is (its tallest crag is only 60 metres (195 feet) above sea level).

From the earliest days of photography, as far back as 1856, the Mount has been a favourite subject and is still photographed in the summer season many thousands of times every day. A number of elegant and historical drawings and engravings have helped to chart its development, some of which can still be seen on display in the castle. The image of the Mount is a symbol not only of The National Trust but also of West Penwith and the whole of Cornwall, an instantly recognisable emblem which speaks of holiday, adventure, summer and romance to the visitor, and more simply of home to Cornish expatriates.

It has more complex resonances too. St Michael's Mount stands at the confluence of several major ley-lines, the mystical straight lines said to link places of supernatural power, often high places dedicated to St Michael. Other religions based on pre-Christian beliefs find the Mount an influential and holy place, a centre of unseen strength and magic. On a less serious note, it also brings to life the lost worlds of fairy stories, and people encountering it for the first time are astonished to see a vision from their earliest imaginings sitting solidly in the middle of a quiet blue sea.

The Mount has its own mythology, mostly concerning the giant Cormoran who lived there and whiled away the days harassing the local populace and quarrelling with other giants. Cormoran is said to have built the Mount, aided by his much put-upon wife who collected the rocks for him. When she failed to notice through her weariness that a hole had been worn in her giant apron and a rock (Chapel Rock, of course) had slipped through, he lost his temper and put her to a violent end. Despite his dire qualities, it is hard not to feel sorry that the brave young hero Jack tricked the giant into rushing into a pit to his doom, thereby bringing the fabulous race of giants to an end.

To journey to the Mount is to walk with ghosts. Countless numbers of people have crossed the 600 metres from the mainland to the island, some bent on conquest, some on trade, some on worship and others, as today, simply curious. You still ascend by the path taken by a thousand years of singing pilgrims; by Bernard le Bec, the first French Abbot; by Robert, Count of Mortain; by Perkin Warbeck and his famously beautiful wife; by Charles II; by Drake and Howard; by Hopton and Fairfax; by families of Bassetts and St Aubyns in good times and bad; by John Opie; by Queen Victoria and Prince Albert; by Edward VII; perhaps by Cormoran and his unhappy spouse; and by other feet of unknown men and women from the mists of prehistory.

All found that the Mount drew them in a way that none of them could explain. Those who have grown up with it are still sometimes struck to silence and pause in their daily round when the light catches it in an unexpected way, and it can take their breath away too. It has something more than can be explained by artist, scholar or historian, or anyone; a quality which can only be described as... magic.